It's Called: "North Carolina"

Ed Caram

It's Called: **"North Carolina"** by Ed Caram

ISBN: 9780615362076

Library of Congress Control Number: 2010903918

Permanent Printing Ltd.
Printed in China

I ain't doin' quite as well as I expected
but then I never really expected I would.

90% ATTITUDE
10% ABILITY

JAMES A GRAHAM

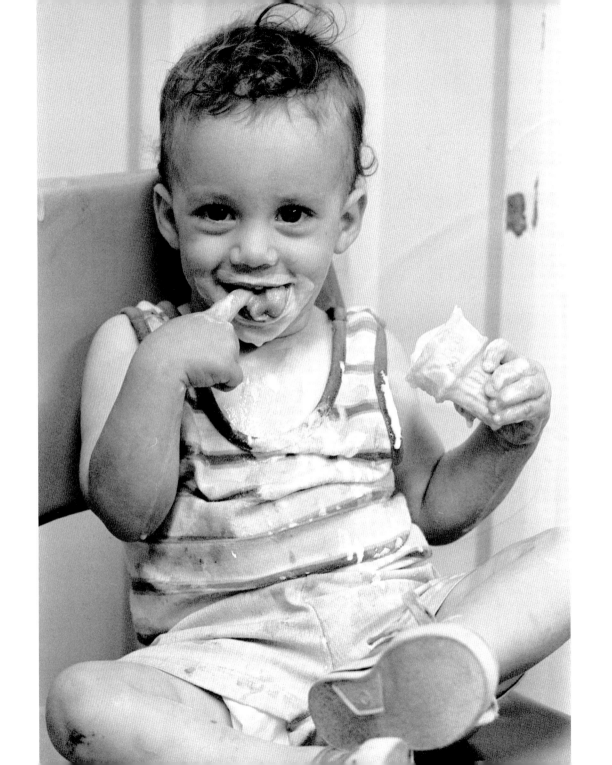

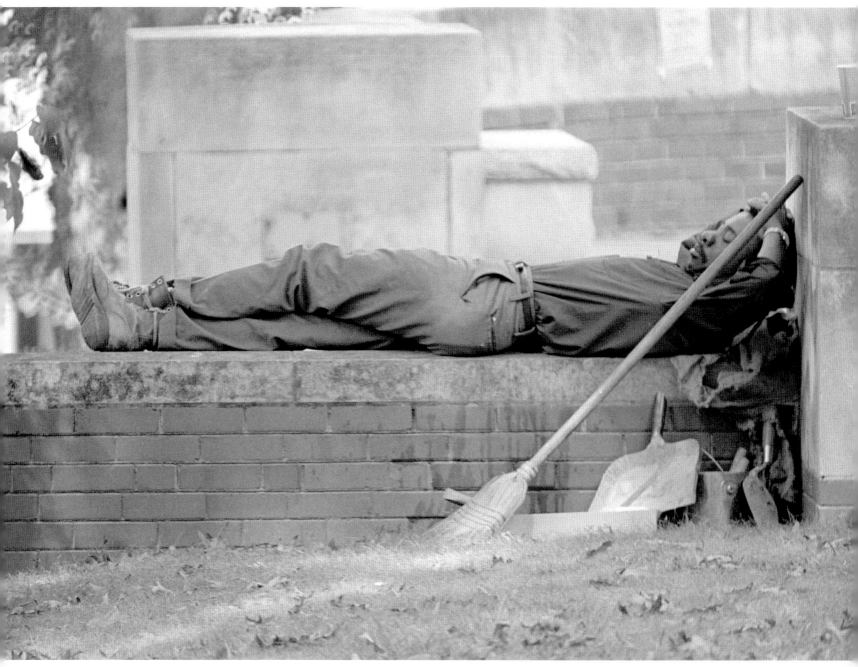

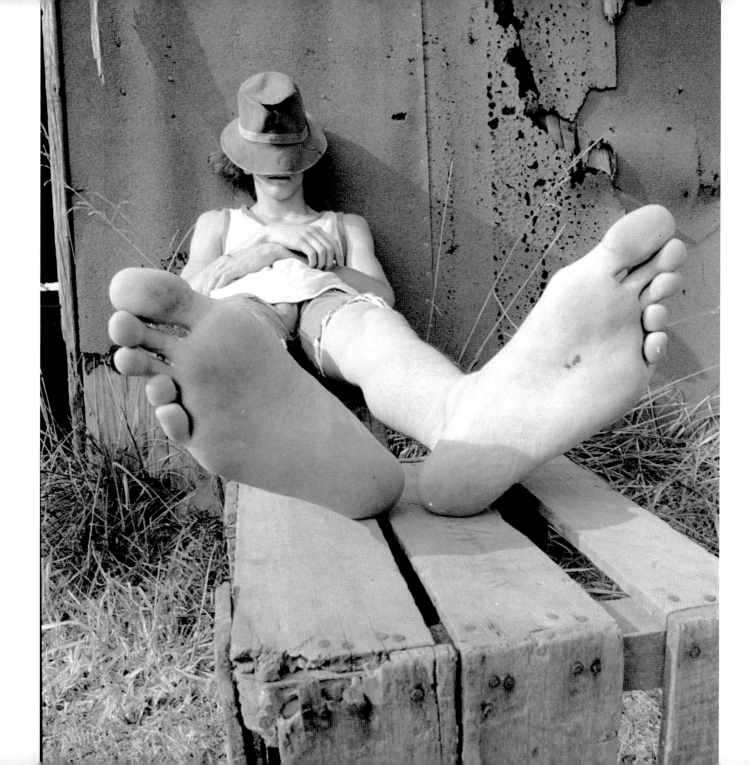

PICTURE NOTES

People ask where these various photos were made. Identifying
each and every photo by location would defeat the purpose of
this photo essay. This collection is supposed to illustrate North
Carolina and its people. The photos should be able to make
the viewer wonder whether they were made where they live.
They represent the pleasant, nice place that I like, the North
Carolina that appeals to me.

To satisfy some of the curious, **some** of the counties that are
represented are Duplin, Wake, Johnston, Warren, Iredell,
Surry, Rockingham, Franklin, Nash, New Hanover, Yadkin,
Wilkes, Davie, Forsyth, Harnett, Jones, Mecklenburg, Wilson,
and Davidson.

The farmer riding the bicycle on the title page is Willie Worrell
of Duplin County. The beauty queen being crowned is at a Miss
North Carolina Pageant. Newly elected Lt. Gov. Jimmy Green
is the man being kissed by his wife.

U.S. Senator Jesse Helms is shown several times speaking on
election night when he won in 1972 and also while campaigning.
The man speaking to the assembled crowd and taking the oath
of office is Gov. Jim Hunt.

Bobby Cave is lifting the tobacco in the tobacco barn in Dobson.
Steve Worrell is holding the two live pigs.

U.S. Senator Sam Ervin is shown speaking with the hand
gesture at a rally in Raleigh. Commissioner of Agriculture
Jim Graham is shown at his desk with the mule picture in the
background.

The old church is at Shotwell.

Tommy Bender is shown with his brother Sam at their home
on their farm near Ridgeway, NC in Warren County with the
Farm Bureau sign in the picture. Elizabeth Worrell is hanging
the clothes in Duplin County.

The pictures of the politicing and politicians were picked to
show the pleasant hometown style of North Carolina
campaigning. These are some of the picture IDs.

I want to show a pleasant happy way of life and people in a
place called North Carolina.

Ed Caram